HOW TO DEAL WITH DIFFICULT PEOPLE

ANNE MULHALL

ASSET BOOKS LTD., DORKING, SURREY RH4 2TU, UNITED KINGDOM

YOUR PROBLEM OR MINE?

HOW TO DEAL WITH 'DIFFICULT' PEOPLE'

ANNE MULHALL

©1995 Asset Books Ltd.,
1 Paper Mews, 330 High Street
Dorking, Surrey RH4 2TU

All rights reserved.

No part of this publication may be reproduced, stored in a retrieval system, or transmitted in any form or by any means, electronic, mechanical, photocopying, recording or otherwise without the written permission of the copyright holders. This book may not be sold, lent, hired out or otherwise dealt with in the course of trade of supply in any form of binding other than that in which it is published without the prior permission of the publishers.

A catalogue record for this book is available from the British Library.

ISBN 1 900179 01 6

Printed and bound in Great Britain by Prisma Press

CONTENTS

Chapter 1: INTRODUCTION	1
Chapter 2: DIFFICULT PEOPLE	8
Who are they?	8
Why are they difficult?	9
Are we all difficult?	10
What to do with a problem relationship	10
Summary	12
CHAPTER 3: CONVENTIONAL APPROACHES	13
Management theory and social psychology	13
Types of difficult people	14
Strategies for dealing with difficult people	17
A general strategy for handling difficult people	18
Summary	23
CHAPTER 4: AN ALTERNATIVE PERSPECTIVE	24
Other ways of looking at the world	24
Cultural relativism	27
Explanations vs. understandings	29
Summary	30
CHAPTER 5: CHANGING THE LABEL	32
Labelling	32
Contested knowledge and being difficult	33
Changing the label	36
Summary	38
CHAPTER 6: DIFFICULT INTERACTIONS AND DEALING WITH THEM	39
Moving on from individualism to co-operation	39
The significance of context	41
In place of the other	44
Summary	46
CHAPTER 7: A PLAN FOR ACTION	47
Listening techniques	47
Synectics©	49
Summary	54

CHAPTER 8: CONCLUSIONS   55

REFERENCES   59

FURTHER READING   60

CHAPTER 1: INTRODUCTION

Throughout every walk of life we encounter people we judge to be 'difficult' - the 'impossible teenager', the 'intrusive neighbour', the 'domineering parent-in-law'. These people seem to inhabit all areas of our lives. We come away from encounters with them feeling bitter, angry, hurt or simply frustrated. Why does he or she always get to me? Why can't I think of the right things to say at the time? Why does the same thing keep happening every time we meet? Reassuringly perhaps, most of us go through these thoughts - often on a daily basis! Which of us has not got their 'hit list' of people they would summarily dismiss from work, or banish from the sport's club committee, if only we were in charge?

Sometimes the problem of difficult people seems to dominate, causing stress and anxiety in our working and social lives, a feeling of disillusionment and surrender. Although there is no doubt that we meet difficult people in all aspects of our lives, it is in the workplace where some of our most difficult encounters with others take place. Why should this be? I would suggest that the special problem of 'difficult' people in the workplace stems from its culture. Culture is the system of shared rules and meanings by which we shape our particular world. Culture tells us how to view the world, but more important to the point here, it tells us how to **act** in our world. The culture of the workplace places extra restraint on the strategies which we might feasibly use in dealing with difficult people. Yelling at our partner, the children, or the cat is rather more socially acceptable than letting fly with your work colleagues. All of us may be 'allowed' one such outburst, but generally this type of reaction is unacceptable.

We all know that different cultures have different characteristics, and these are commonly used when comedians or cartoonists compose stereotypic images of 'foreigners'. The foods we eat, the way we dress, the systems we use to organise family and work - these are the more obvious trappings of culture, but there are other, more subtle, themes. Recently, anthropologists have turned their attention from studying exotic cultures to describing matters closer to home. One of the ideas they have put forward is that self-control is a dominant symbol of Western societies. Self-discipline has become the supreme virtue, the bedrock of 'character' and achievement. It has formed the foundation for a culture of professionalism. We must be seen to be in control. In control of our work-load, our subordinates, our duties as a mother, our lives. This has implications both for the sort of strategies that we might use when dealing with difficult people and for the common purpose of what constitutes a 'difficult' person.

What is increasingly obvious is that, for many of us, our methods of coping with the people we perceive to be difficult are frustratingly inadequate and that, although we have difficult interactions at home, these are probably magnified in the work situation.

Furthermore, the current economic climate in Western societies is conspiring to make the situation worse rather than better. In an economic crisis, the discipline and control associated with work are made ever more obvious. The UK has, over the last ten years, witnessed a tremendous upheaval in the organisation and running of service industries such as education, health and social care, local government and transport. Many of these have either been 'privatised' or re-organised to run along business lines. Those working in these fields have, therefore, been forced to undergo a series of changes to their working practices and management. Very often this has resulted in an obligation to mould together disparate groups of professionals who may hold differing philosophies towards, say, health care or education and its management.

For example, the now famous Griffiths' report (Department of Health and Social Security, 1983) introduced the concept of general management into the National Health Service (NHS). The subsequent development of the 'internal market' put further pressure on hospitals, GP practices, community health centres and the like to revise the way in which they operated. Patients have become customers (or clients) and health care organisations must, increasingly, operate along the lines of competitive business. Naturally many of these changes have been effected and sustained by administrators trained in business studies, accountancy and so on. The re-organisations have, therefore, tended to marginalise health care professionals, such as doctors and nurses, minimising their contribution to the organisation and management of hospitals and other bodies. The NHS has thereby become dominated by a large cadre of general managers.

This development was, perhaps, only to be expected given the nature of the re-organisations. However it is not difficult to see how such changes, both in the NHS and the many other service industries affected by such cultural change, have caused conflict between different professional groups. The goals, strategies and values of, say, teachers, doctors or social workers are frequently at odds with the requirements of running an effective and efficient business. Although it would be crass to suggest that the latter objective is the only aim of general managers, their ideology and working practices do differ in significant ways from these other professionals. It should come as no great surprise that these developments have engendered a culture where, increasingly, each working day appears to be dominated with trying to 'work around' difficult people.

Many professionals have also witnessed an increasing emphasis on providing value for money in an era when resources are becoming increasingly scarce. Alongside this have been initiatives aimed at measuring individual performance through the use of audit and quality control initiatives. Job performance and output must be speeded up whilst wages are held down. Similar strategies have focused on organisations to produce 'league tables' of, for example, hospitals, schools or universities.

While, in one sense, these are welcome initiatives, the pressure on individuals to 'perform' to certain standards (which, in many cases, may be set outwith the respective professions or organisations) brings its own attendant problems. Personal and collective competence is questioned as issues such as job security and a changing culture of work come to the fore. However we cope with the situation, none of us relishes the prospect of being judged. The externally mediated pressures, such as those which have faced many service industries recently, may engender an increasingly hostile work culture wherein 'difficult people' seem to be encountered with depressing frequency. Yet it is during such times of mounting scrutiny and accountability that the ability to maximise inter-personal relationships and to develop cohesive teams whose members are loyal to each other, becomes vital. Strategies for dealing with difficult people and difficult relationships become increasingly essential as each individual 'plots' his or her way through often uncharted, and frequently hostile, territory.

Anyone who has browsed through the local book-shop or library cannot have remained unaware of the proliferation of books and manuals discussing or describing workplace practices and/or strategies. This is quite a recent trend. The study of workplace practice and management expanded in the second half of the 20th century, starting in the USA but rapidly spreading to the UK and Europe. The problem for early investigators in this field was trying to find some existing theories or ideas on which they could base and expand their own work. Many studies therefore 'borrowed' extensively from other disciplines, in particular economics and social psychology.

Developing alongside this business academia has been an upsurge in books, manuals and courses that provide more practical guidance to solving the dilemmas which we all face in our everyday work. Not unnaturally, the material within these is often based on psychology and, in particular, the ways in which people behave in certain situations. Strategies for dealing with these situations - be they difficult people, trying to effect change, building up teams and so on - are thereby devised to meet certain predicted behaviour and outcomes.

Using this approach a range of difficult people, for example the 'Sherman tank' or the 'Sniper', has been proposed and the appropriate strategies for dealing with these types have been put forward (Bransom, 1981). Some of these will be discussed later in the book.

This is not, however, the only way by which we might think about difficult people and how to deal with them. Putting aside the focus on individuals and their behaviour, the approach adopted by psychology, an alternative approach suggests that a social system, such as your workplace, is a complex phenomenon made up not only of individuals but also the environment and 'atmosphere' in which you work. Furthermore, all these elements will be interrelated and dependent upon each other. Change one part of the system and you may well change another. Looking at things in this way might suggest that the solutions to the problem of difficult people will only be found through an examination of the context of social interactions. It is not just you and your difficult person, but the complex social milieu in which you interact which must be determined. This view also lays heavy emphasis on 'unearthing' the meaning, rather than the function, of interactions. In other words in discovering **why** things happen rather than concentrating only on **what** happens

This book explores both these approaches to dealing with difficult people. Although focusing in the main on practical issues we will, on occasions delve a little deeper to explore some of the theoretical background involved. These little excursions into theory will be quite light and should provide you with a more thoughtful insight into the problem of difficult people, and how we might cope with it.

Although each chapter 'stands alone' a logical argument concerning difficult people and how we should cope with them is developed as the text progresses. This continuity, and the relative brevity of the text, suggests that you should work progressively through the book in a logical sequence. Each chapter contains a number of activities, usually for working on alone. It is strongly recommended that you attempt to find the time to undertake at least some of these. They are not particularly taxing but should, hopefully, help you to understand the points being made more clearly.

The book does not set out to provide all the answers. Sometimes you may find the suggestions either inapplicable to you or unworkable in the set of circumstances in which you find yourself. Throughout the book, therefore, the emphasis is on self-development, to help you to evolve your own particular model for dealing with difficult interactions. A guide which will help you to understand more clearly why you find some people 'difficult' and others 'easy'. Perhaps most important of all, however, is for you to stop and reflect on yourself and your interactions with others. Productive reflection on the way we work and interact with others is a valuable, but under used, tool. It costs us nothing and can yield rich rewards. So don't just read the text and complete the activities, develop an 'attitude', a state of mind, which will see you through the most testing of encounters with 'difficult' people.

CHAPTER 2: DIFFICULT PEOPLE

Who are they?

Composing a list of 'difficult people' would not involve many of us in either a great deal of time or in great feats of mental effort. But stop and think about your situation - at work or at home. Would you, your colleagues and family come up with the same names, the same difficult people? Does a small section of the work-force, or the same family member, continually cause problems in their relations with others? Are my difficult people your difficult people? The answers to these questions probably depend on the context of any particular encounter. When does the interaction occur? Who else is there? Where do these difficult encounters happen?

Although the answers are important, American research has suggested that approximately 10% of people are consistently tough to deal with, or difficult. This information comes from the work of Robert Bransom, a behavioural scientist who spent seven years observing how people dealt with difficult encounters, both at work and at home.

> **ACTIVITY:**
> Try making your own list of people who, over the years, you have regarded as difficult to handle. Doing this is your first step in taking a more rational approach to learning to deal with difficult people, to stop acting impulsively, on the spur of the moment, when you're angry or hurt. It is a step towards cool reflection.

Probably the names on your list will change as people move in and out of your life, but some may remain for years or decades as a perpetual reminder of your inability to 'get the better of them'! In our social lives, it is usually possible to gradually 'shed' such people from our circle of acquaintances. However, close relatives or partners pose particular problems that may tax all our diplomatic skills. It is at work, however, where some of the most persistent and frustrating interactions with difficult people occur.

As job security becomes a myth of the past, and opportunities for changing jobs diminish, the imperative to 'fit in' and progress in one specific job or institution becomes inescapable. Ten years ago, when unemployment was at relatively modest levels, work-force mobility was a realistic aspiration. However, it is now less likely that we will be able to change jobs and 'escape' from our difficult people. Furthermore, few of us can ignore the implications that a poor appraisal of our work efforts may bring; the way in which we handle difficult people may have a direct bearing on our work performance and subsequent appraisal.

Why are they difficult?

Recognising difficult people causes few problems, but what makes them difficult? You could easily add to the list you have just made a second column of the characteristics of those you have identified, which anger, frustrate or simply defy your comprehension. Again you will probably identify certain features that you find difficult to handle in anyone. It might be irrational anger, a patronising attitude, a disregard for the feelings of others and so on. What is harder to decide is whether it is just a certain trait about a person that makes them difficult to handle, or a whole array of characteristics which interact to produce a difficult personality (from your point of view).

Can we recognise certain people as always being difficult, or does the context in which we interact with them give meaning to the encounter? Do we always react in specific ways to the challenge of a difficult interaction? For example, nurses often speak of 'difficult patients', usually those who are most demanding of their time, and most critical of the services offered. But would these same people be considered difficult once they had regained their health and moved outside the hospital environment? Are the characteristics of 'difficulty' ingrained, or do they depend on time and place? These are important questions because they may determine the potential strategies through which difficult encounters might be eased.

Are we all difficult?

This discussion leads naturally to consideration of whether, in reality, we are all difficult at certain times and in certain places? The common sense answer seems to be 'yes'. Each and every one of us has, at times, caused difficulties in our relationships with others, be they spouses, mothers, work colleagues, employees, or casual acquaintances who we encounter as we go about our daily life. The tendency to regard others as difficult whilst failing to recognise our own foibles, stems from a natural tendency for self-survival. We are all rational within our own worlds.

What to do with a problem relationship

Which one of us has not, on the way home from a frustrating day at work, imagined the strategies that we are going to use to deal (usually punitively) with those people with whom we have had less than satisfactory encounters? Be it the boss who continually undermines our confidence, the 'helpful' colleague who seems to question every plan we attempt to activate, or the car park attendant who repeatedly gives our space away if we arrive more than a few minutes after the appointed hour. Frustratingly, such plans rarely, if ever, seem to be successful and the same cycle of interaction and conflict repeats itself on subsequent occasions.

The question of what to do with a relationship problem is, however refreshingly simple. You can either:

- Leave it alone

or

- Do something about it.

Naturally both of these courses of action will involve certain consequences. Leaving it alone indicates that, on balance, your preference is to live with the problem relationship, coping with its potential outcomes in a variety of ways. Although this may be seen as a failure to face up to things, inactivity is often the optimum strategy.

There are other outlets for exasperation, anger and humiliation - use them. Go jogging, swim 50 lengths, let off steam with an understanding friend or partner, write everything down. Any activity that exorcises your negativity, as long as it is not to the detriment of others, may be worth a try. In a sense, the decision to do nothing about a problem relationship is doing something. You have decided to endure it, at least for the time being. There are however, more proactive strategies that you may decide to employ. These are based on the belief that, by changing your behaviour, or more specifically the way you interact with the difficult person, a better outcome will ensue. Such strategies are often grounded in research derived from studies looking at the psychology of interpersonal relations and the problems of social perception - the factors affecting the way we see others.

> **ACTIVITY:**
>
> Keep a note of your angry moments. What incidents triggered them off? What feelings did you have? These might be physical feelings such as sickness or headache, or more mental feelings such as anxiety or jealousy.

Summary

This chapter has outlined some ideas about difficult people by asking 'Who are they'? Why are they difficult? Are we all difficult? It has initiated our quest for a solution by suggesting an initial strategy for dealing with a problem relationship - do nothing or do something. The next chapter expands on this by exploring the theoretical background underpinning studies of social behaviour. We then examine some practical steps for dealing with difficult people based on this approach.

CHAPTER 3: CONVENTIONAL APPROACHES

Management Theory and Social Psychology

Much of what has been written about modern management relies heavily on theory and research drawn from two established social sciences, namely economics and social psychology. However, in the field of relationships and the strategies we employ when interacting with others, not surprisingly it is social psychology that has made the greatest contribution. Before moving on to discuss possible strategies for dealing with difficult people it is, therefore, important to briefly explore the basis of social psychology and the sort of information that we might expect it to provide.

Social psychology concerns individuals and, more specifically, their behaviour. It is also an objective science which strives towards measurement and prediction. Essentially, social psychology is the scientific study of social behaviour and thought. The knowledge within this discipline is gained through empirical (i.e. based on observation) methods of testing and formulating theories and suggests that there are certain, perhaps universal, patterns to the way we think and act which, in some cases, can be measured and predicted in advance. By observing people in everyday social settings we may unearth patterns to their interactions thus answering questions about what controls and regulates their activity.

There is however, an alternative view. This suggests that the scientific approach, such as that taken by much of psychology, with its emphasis on laws and predictability, is inadequate and misleading when applied to the social world of human beings (the 'real' world). The complexities of the real world cannot be broken down into simple components for study, but must be viewed as a whole.

Thus research, and the philosophies underpinning it, offer us two ways of thinking about the world and, therefore, two ways of trying to investigate it. This chapter focuses on the first approach, what it tells us about the way people interact, and suggests some of the strategies that might be used when trying to change the nature of these interactions.

Types of difficult people

Using some of the methods of the behavioural sciences in general, and social psychology in particular, different types of difficult people can be identified and grouped together in categories.

Robert Bransom spent seven years observing groups of people trying to solve problems. He noted that although some people were difficult others managed to cope with many of the difficulties that these people threw at them. From this he began to recognise different types of difficult people and, more importantly, he identified the coping mechanisms that seemed to be the most effective in dealing with them. The rest of this section will consider some of these types and outline some of the coping strategies which Bransom discovered were useful.

Hostile Aggressives

Bransom gives us some evocative labels for the difficult people found in this group - Sherman Tanks, Snipers and Exploders. They mow down everything in their path, creep up on you unexpectedly, and act in an unpredictable way. Such people need to be in control of their surroundings and fellow human beings, they are aggressive and generally hostile. If their plans are thwarted, or even questioned, they may shout and intimidate others, or attempt to 'put them in their place'. They are rulers who don't like change unless they instigate it, and are quick to anger.

Perhaps I've been fortunate, but despite the evidence that such types exist, I've seldom encountered such people in my working environment. This may reflect the type of people who enter professions such as teaching, nursing or medicine; alternatively it may be a sign of a more general trend towards tolerance and democracy which society as a whole has undergone since Bransom's research in the 1970s.

Critical Advice Givers/Negativists

Experience tells us that, although there may not be many people who fit the previous category, critical advice givers abound. In their most blatant form they are easily spotted; they are honour-bound to produce a counter-argument to each new idea that is put forward. Potential solutions to any problem will always have a flaw in their eyes and, despite lengthy discussions, they usually remain firmly entrenched in their original opinions. Where such people are most difficult to deal with is when they are able to back up their arguments with a barrage of facts and figures, confidently presented at precisely the right moment in any negotiation. A point worth noting here is that they may actually be the 'real experts' and, despite their condescending manner, they might hold the key to your problem

Negativists are less easy to detect and more detrimental to any attempt at problem solving as they often mask their negative approach with a cloak of helpfulness - 'Yes that's a good idea but ....'. Listening to them may lead to fruitless discussions which result in very little change or improvement in working practices. In addition, Bransom suggests, they may 'deflate the optimism' of those around them. They gradually 'grind you down' until you begin to stop thinking about, or trying to initiate, any innovations.

Many working environments are currently undergoing a period of rapid change which has led to widespread lowering of morale and a loss of personal confidence in the ability to act to change things for the better. In this climate, negativists may flourish and be particularly destructive both to individual and organisational integrity.

Unresponsives

Compared to the hostile aggressives and the negativist one might imagine that unresponsives are easy to handle. Nothing could be further from the truth! Unresponsives are those people who sit at the back of meetings and never contribute even when 'pushed'. Any request for a response will be met either with silence or a monosyllabic answer. The problem is that you will not know why they're silent, do they violently disagree with some plan you have put forward and will they, therefore, make no attempt to implement it? Have they something vital and worth-while to add to the debate, but are too shy to speak out? Their very interaction with you (i.e. no interaction) makes devising a strategy to deal with them more effectively extremely difficult.

Agreers/Delayers

This group has the good sense to know that most people like being liked. They will, therefore, go out of their way to agree with your proposals and are always very supportive and enthusiastic. They themselves have a strong desire to be approved of and to fit in with those with whom they work. This will, of course, dictate that they are not only agreeing with your point of view, but probably everyone else's as well! Such people may, therefore, agree to a gamut of commitments few of which will be followed through.

> **ACTIVITY:**
> So far we have identified four broad groups of 'difficult' people. There are, of course, other variants on these. You might like to spend some time thinking whether the people who you find difficult are included in these descriptions.
> If you come up with some other types, try to identify the essential features that characterise them, the messages they send out and, more importantly, why you think they send these particular messages.

Strategies for dealing with difficult people

Before discussing potential strategies for dealing with the different types of difficult people identified here, it is important to explore the mechanisms, which should all else fail, we can use to protect our self-worth and ensure that we don't become victims of the behaviour of others if it is, in fact, unreasonable. It is relatively easy to slip into the role of the 'victim' or the 'abused' and most of us have assumed one of these roles at some stage in our lives. Listening to, and asking advice of ourselves is central to maintaining both our inner composure and the outer skin with which we face the world. We can seek advice and counsel but, in the end, we're on our own.

A simple and effective strategy for achieving inner well-being is to affirm your self-worth through repeating statements appropriate to you and your goals. These positive affirmations equate with the rights that you and every other human being have a claim to. Examples include:

- The right to be successful in your life and work - 'I'm successful in the way I live and no-one has absolute power over me.'
- The right to refuse requests - 'From hereon I won't do anything I don't want to do.'
- The right to make your own decisions - 'I'm free to live in any way that I decide.'
- The right to request the things you want - 'I have the courage, strength and ability to make the changes that are required.'

We could choose many other statements to express both our fundamental rights and the feelings associated with them. Some build up our confidence, some calm us down, some deal with negativity. If you are suffering from an excess of difficult people, or are just generally 'feeling the strain' make a list of statements to help you regain your inner self-esteem and confidence. Try to set aside a time every day to repeat them once or twice.

A general strategy for handling difficult people

So far we have seen how the study of behaviour can lead to the recognition of certain categories of difficult people and so help to develop strategies to deal with them. These, however, depend largely on your own efforts. Firstly, to recognise what is going on in a particular situation, and secondly, to change the way in that you approach the encounter. Although there are specific ways of dealing effectively with each of the categories, a general strategy of coping successfully with any type of difficult person can be proposed. ESCAPE! from this unproductive and damaging interaction and reformulate it so that you accomplish more from your future encounters (see Figure 3.1).

Figure 3.1   ESCAPE!

> ### ESCAPE!
> **EXAMINE** the situation - is it really a problem or are you having an 'off day'?
>
> **STOP** dreaming that the situation will improve or disappear.
>
> **CATEGORISE** the behaviour that you observe from an objective standpoint.
>
> **ACQUIRE** a strategy for coping with the interaction. How can you change things to ensure a more productive outcome the next time you meet?
>
> **PUT** your plan into action. Rehearse it and implement it at a good time (i.e. when the person concerned will be most receptive).
>
> **EVALUATE** how successful your coping plan has been. Did you get a more positive response? Do you feel better about the way you are interacting? If not, try to think through why this might be.

Dealing with Hostile Aggressives

The natural reactions to an encounter with any one of the trio of hostile aggressives are feelings of anger, helplessness, mortification and confusion. There may be an almost overwhelming desire to 'get back at them'. To handle these people effectively:

- Don't argue or attack them, but hold your ground
- Control your own inevitable anger
- Listen to them, but don't put yourself down or give in
- Acknowledge the sniper's cutting remark, but don't laugh, take it seriously
- Arrange a break if possible
- Attempt to meet in private when things cool down.

Dealing with Critical Advice Givers/Negativists

These are the people who think they know it all - sometimes they do, but more often they don't, they are simply good orators with thick skins and an inflated sense of their own worth. They think they are superior to you and let you know it. Both critical advice givers and negativists can undermine your security and self-esteem. They may make you feel helpless, unknowledgeable or even childlike. To handle these people effectively:

- Be prepared - they will be!
- Listen to what they say and ask for related ideas which might apply more directly to the problem in hand
- Give credit where credit is due

- If advice is faulty calmly delineate the correct facts but don't be too dogmatic
- Use their negativism to spot the genuinely weak points of your own arguments
- Negativism can be addictive - don't fall into the sympathetic depression trap
- Take action on your own account (i.e. essentially disregard them).

Dealing with Unresponsives

The messages that unresponsives send can be most destructive in terms of maintaining our equilibrium. 'Take care, you can't predict how I will respond.' 'By keeping silent I remain in control.' 'Leave me alone and you won't have to confront these silences'. This leads to feelings of discomfort, guilt and possibly anger and frustration at one's inability to get these people to open up and contribute. Unlike the other two groups the unresponsives can be baffling and their motives may be well hidden. To handle these people effectively:

- Ask open questions - Where? Why? How? etc..
- Learn to cope with the inevitable silence, be comfortable with it
- Use an open friendly expression indicating that you are waiting for an answer and will continue to wait
- Don't take the responsibility yourself (i.e. don't jump in to fill the silence, or believe that the problem is yours)

- End the interaction on a positive note, but follow them up for a private discussion.

Dealing with Agreers/Delayers

Everything sounds good to these people, but nothing ever happens. They continually stall and delay on both decisions and actions to which you thought you had their agreement. This puts you in an awkward position whereby it is difficult to criticise them or apply any pressure because they are often very personable and supportive. This may result in feelings of confusion and guilt on your part. To handle such people effectively:

- Assist them to identify priorities
- Be appreciative and personal with them - they need your approval
- Open the way for them to disagree
- Collaborate with them and follow through on any decision that is made.

None of these plans for managing difficult people more effectively should be regarded as the last word on the subject, or the only route through which you might achieve success. They are merely suggestions that have been found to work based on other people's experience and research. You need to adapt and adopt these strategies to suit your individual needs at different times and different places.

Remember also that, whatever the type of difficult person you are trying to deal with, at first most of the work at improving your relationship will have to come from your side. Many commentators agree that persistence may be required in achieving the desired result.

Summary

This chapter has examined some of the ways in which the behavioural sciences have provided the information to help and to guide our interactions with difficult people. It has indicated that it is possible to categorise people into groups with similar characteristics. Similarly, research has demonstrated that there are certain strategies which, more often than not, will work effectively in helping us to cope with our encounters with different types of difficult people. All we need to do is recognise the type and apply the solution!

Such strategies are not designed to change or 'get rid of' difficult people, but to enable you to achieve more from your interactions with them. The next chapter will take a radically different stance by providing an alternative way of viewing difficulties between people.

CHAPTER 4: AN ALTERNATIVE PERSPECTIVE - Other ways of looking at the world

In considering the possible ways of dealing with difficult people it is important that the different approaches used in research contributing to our understanding of difficult relationships are considered as they may offer us alternative strategies we could use to address the problem.

The last chapter discussed how psychology may help our understanding of relationships and showed that research based on psychology has particular characteristics and aims associated with the way in which the area of interest is perceived. In other words, researchers use methods consistent with the way that they 'see' the subject of their study. This type of research is often called 'scientific' as it follows the 'scientific method' and relies on careful observation and collection of data, often in the form of numbers, from which laws and theories can be derived and which, in turn, can be used to predict events.

Such research tends to focus on a single behavioural characteristic (such as anxiety, fear or anger) providing a narrow view of that characteristic. Such characteristics are often measured using some sort of numerical scale. It is believed that the methods used to collect and verify data mean that such work is free from the opinions (biases) of the researcher so that the results from one study can be used to predict what might happen in other groups of people.

Other approaches adopt a broader view looking at the 'whole picture', the person, his lifestyle, where he works, who he is friendly with, what he does at home, etc.. In other words, they suggest that there are always multiple views of any situation and these cannot be separated out for investigation. In any social situation, including difficult encounters, many things are happening at once.

The difference between these approaches can, perhaps, be seen more clearly by considering the difference between seeing a photograph of a goal being scored and watching a video of the entire match. The latter reveals the context in which the goal was scored and we can see the factors contributing to it. We have seen the event in its 'natural state' rather than in a 'freeze frame'; we have seen the 'whole picture'.

Researchers who are looking for the whole picture will make every effort not to change or control that which is being studied. They want to study things or people in their natural state, as they actually occur. This is why such studies are often termed **naturalism** or **interpretism**. Such researchers also believe that meaning is not fixed and the values and context of that being studied must be acknowledged. In other words, they suggest that the meaning given to a situation can change depending on who is observing it, when it happens, who is involved and so on.

This way of looking at things is epitomised by **systems theory** which states that all the parts of any social system are intertwined and related. We cannot, for example, try to investigate bullying at school by asking those who are bullied to complete a psychological questionnaire. We need to recognise that the teachers, other children or the structure and organisation of the school may all play a part. In other words, the sum of the system is more than its component parts, it cannot be torn apart into small pieces for study. These two ways of looking at the world are summarised in Table 4.1 (page 26).

TABLE 4.1   The characteristics of 'science' and naturalism

SCIENCE	NATURALISM
Hard	Soft
Objective	Subjective
Narrow focus	Broad focus
Controlled	Shared interpretation
Reductionist	Holistic
Looking for cause and effect relationships	Looking for meaning
Generalisable	Unique

ACTIVITY:

You might like to think about which of these views you are most sympathetic to.

- Do you like the hard objective information which science produces - lots of facts and figures?

Or

- Are you more swayed by descriptions, personal stories, biographies and so on?

The choice you make is likely to influence the sorts of strategies that you will feel most comfortable with when trying to improve your relationships with difficult people. Broadly speaking, if you favour the scientific approach then categorising people and applying a strategy for dealing with them as discussed in Chapter 3 may be for you but, if you feel more sympathy to the second approach, read on!

These two ways of trying to investigate the social world provide different perspectives on society and the relationships within it. The first, adopted by many psychologists, suggests that, by observing and categorising the way people act, it is possible to make predictions about particular groups and so select certain strategies to deal with them.

The second embraces a more 'holistic' approach suggesting that the intricacies of social action can only be revealed by examining the context in which events and interactions occur through the 'real life' accounts of those involved. This chapter explores how this approach can also help us understand how people interact and so how we can optimise our relationships, particularly with those we perceive as 'difficult'.

What is of interest is the wish to see 'things' through the 'eye of the beholder'. Rather than trying to observe and categorise behaviour independently, researchers try to discover, often in people's own words, what it is like to be for example, a patient with terminal cancer, a university lecturer, or a child on their first day at school. Information is often gathered by spending long periods of time with the people concerned, talking to them, writing notes about their surroundings, describing their day, etc.. These long descriptions are clearly very different to the types of objective evidence used by other scientists.

Cultural Relativism

Integral to naturalism is the idea that the perspective of both those being studied and the researcher must be brought out into the open. That is, the researcher must acknowledge his own attitudes and beliefs and open them for all to see. Having done this, he or she must then try to decide how they may have influenced the situation they were trying to study.

Equally there is the notion that we are all rational in our own worlds. **Our** world makes sense to **us**, and we act in it accordingly. **You** may not understand **why** your boss acts as he does but, for him, his interactions with you make perfect sense. This picks up on a current theme in modern social anthropology, that of **cultural relativism**, which holds that the customs and practices of different cultures are equally valid. What is right and wrong, accepted and unaccepted, will vary with time and place - no one culture or individual has the monopoly on the right way to live. We all have our own way of living and, within the limits of our society, we must all recognise this cultural diversity.

ACTIVITY:

Spend some time thinking about the way you see others.
- Are there certain groups or individuals with whom you always seem to have difficulties?
- Write a list of these people and the sorts of things they do which annoy or frustrate you.
- What messages do you think they are sending you and why?

This activity should help you to disentangle both the people and the particular characteristics that you find difficult. It may also unearth some well-suppressed prejudices. Be honest with yourself and try to expose these hidden thoughts - this will make it easier for you to deal with them.

Explanations vs. Understandings

Typically scientific research seeks to establish predictable laws governing the behaviour of individuals and whole societies. It is concerned with explanations and asks such questions as 'What'? and 'How many'? In contrast, naturalism hopes to interpret or to understand what is going on. It is seeking the meaning of events from the perspective of those involved. The sorts of question which arise here are 'Why?', 'How come?' This perspective, therefore, is less concerned with labelling and categorising behaviour or interactions, but rather tries to understand them. It recognises that any interaction between two human beings will have particular significance for both of those involved. Thus a scientist and naturalist would approach the study of the way people interact within an organisation, and more specifically, the difficult situations that may arise between individuals, in different ways.

The 'scientist' would wish to observe and categorise the behaviour objectively into certain types. The characteristics of each type would be noted and strategies to deal with them would be proposed. The 'naturalist' would be more interested in finding out **why** people behaved as they did in certain encounters. Why does Jane always leave the staff meeting feeling put down, demotivated and lonely? Is it something to do with her interactions with other members of staff and, if so, what leads to these states of being? What meanings and interpretations does Jane put on these events? This sort of information often reveals what is going on during an interaction rather than its ultimate outcome. Understanding how we get to a certain outcome is very helpful in determining the different courses of action we might adopt in the future.

This seems to suggest that it may not be helpful to label behaviours, as described in Chapter 3, and assume that, when we come across them again, we will know how to deal with them. Furthermore, the context and environment in which interactions occur would also be important. When and where the interaction took place, the other people present, the events leading to the encounter and the subsequent events that occurred might all be important in trying to understand the dynamics of the exchange which took place. This business of context is important and will be explored further in the next chapter.

ACTIVITY:

Ponder on one relationship that you consider difficult.

Do the same problems keep coming up with this person? Or are there a range of different difficulties, some occurring on one occasion and some on another? Is it the person who is difficult or are you labelling them? Can you avoid the set of circumstances that leads to the difficulty when you encounter this person the next time around?

Summary

This chapter has offered another perspective through which we might view the world by contrasting science with naturalism. By examining the concepts behind these two philosophies we have seen how they may provide, on the one hand, explanations (science) and, on the other, understanding (naturalism). It has also raised the idea that each person's customs and practices, although possibly different from our own, are equally valid.

In the final section the central importance of context to the understanding of interactions was stressed. The next chapter will continue this theme of naturalism to see what it has to offer us. It will pursue the idea that we need to stand back from relationships with difficult people and try to understand **why** they are difficult.

CHAPTER 5: CHANGING THE LABEL

Labelling

Much has been written in both the educational and health care literature about the dangers and difficulties associated with attaching 'labels' to either individuals or groups. Sometimes this practice has been associated with outright prejudice, perhaps in the form of racism, ageism or sexism, but labels have often been historically derived or ingrained into professional practices. For example, implicit in the use of the word 'girl' instead of 'woman', is the idea of immaturity, juvenile behaviour, etc.. It is feminist research that has shown how the continued use of these historically derived words continues to confirm women's place as secondary to men. Similarly nurses have, in the past, described patients by their symptoms or illnesses - the appendicectomy in bed 12, the chronic diabetic at the Thursday clinic, the Down's syndrome in room 4 etc.. Once such labels have been revealed it is not hard to see that not only may they place certain individuals apart from the rest of society but they are also intrinsically depersonalising and insensitive. However, it may take many years, and some insightful research, for such labels to be exposed for what they are.

A researcher from the US illustrated how deeply embedded labels may become by examining how other health care researchers talked about risk factors for AIDS. She noted how, rather than speaking of risky behaviours, such as sharing needles or unprotected sexual intercourse, the researchers fell into the habit of defining particular **groups** as at risk for AIDS so that being, for example, a Haitian or an intravenous drug abuser became a risk factor.

Similarly, a sociologist working in Oxford recorded how midwives used certain stereotypes to guide their interactions with Asian women. When interviewed none of the midwives stated that they disliked Asian clients yet, because of the way that Asian women were unconsciously 'constructed' in the midwive's collective eyes, they were seen as 'difficult patients'. They were characterised as possessing certain behaviours which guided the midwive's responses to them. One of these behaviours concerned a belief that Asians have lower pain thresholds than Europeans. However, instead of alerting health care professionals to the potentially more painful labour that Asians might endure, this had an almost counterproductive effect. Thus, if an Asian was distressed during labour, it was not because they were in pain but because they had a lower pain threshold.

Thus we can see that some labels are very obvious, such as those associated with derogatory racial categories. Other labels may, however, be difficult to recognise and people (such as the midwives and health care researchers) would probably strenuously deny that they were using labels to the detriment of others.

Having stayed with me so far, you might be forgiven for asking what this has to do with dealing with difficult people? The point is that the practice of labelling people - 'the superagreeable', 'the Sherman tank' - may not be in our, or their, best interests. Ask yourself this simple question. Would you like to be labelled in this rather arbitrary and quite often derogatory way?

Contested Knowledge and Being Difficult

It is worth making what is perhaps a diversion, but one which is important, to explore what we consider to be our own knowledge.

You know, or at least you think you know, certain things. How have you come to know these things? Do your colleagues know these things and do they know them in the same way? Now this is, I admit, getting a bit deep but, if you reflect a little, you will realise that, whether you are a teacher, a nurse, a physiotherapist, a doctor or a college lecturer, you will have gathered knowledge from many different sources throughout your life time. Much of this will have been derived from your life experiences, your childhood, your relationships and so on. To put it colloquially, what you learnt at your mother's, or indeed father's, knee.

However, much of our knowledge as adults stems from our education and, if we belong to a professional group, from our training. Further, it is not just factual information - the anatomy of the body, or the psychological stages of development - it is also the system of shared thoughts and ideas about what it is like to be 'a dental nurse', 'a primary school teacher', a 'health care manager', etc.. This system of shared perceptions, rules, and meanings is our culture. Culture tells us both how to **view** the world and how to **act** in it. Thus we expect, say, politicians to dress and act in a certain way and, when they don't, the force of society is brought to bear on their apparent transgression from the 'unwritten rules', they have contravened our expectations.

This idea of culture links with the concept of contested knowledge. All groups, especially professional groups, possess what they consider to be **the** knowledge about a certain situation. It is easy to see then how difficulties between individual members of different professional groups can arise. This is very evident in the traditional schism between nursing and medicine, where each profession jealously guards what it considers to be its 'patch'. Rifts are also often apparent between the lay public and professional. How many times have you been to your child's parents' evening, only to come away frustrated and annoyed because your opinion differed from that of the teacher?

A study of childbirth practises in Northern Canada clearly illustrates the gulf that can exist between the ideas of different individuals, and how this can lead to conflict. The official policy of the Canadian Federal Department of Health and Welfare was that all births should occur in hospital. However, for Inuit women, the risks of childbirth, although not denied, were rather accepted as part of the reality of living in the northern part of Canada in relatively hostile physical territory. The women wanted to give birth locally, and saw it in terms of a real demand for control and also as a highly symbolic gesture. In contrast, the doctors looking after them spoke of the official statistics which indicated greater risks of the baby dying if it was not delivered in a large state hospital.

However, not only did the doctors speak in 'officialdom' they also reverted to personal experience to emphasise their point. The fear of haemorrhage occurring after birth was particularly powerful, and the idea of seeing a woman bleeding to death, and being able to do nothing to help, exerted very strong effects on their views concerning hospital versus community births.

Thus you can see how each 'side' was, in their own way, being 'difficult'. Both groups, mothers and doctors, not only wielded factual information but also more ideological reasons for the particular stance that they adopted. This was **contested knowledge**; both the Inuit women and the doctors knew they were right!

Changing the Label

This chapter has provided three new thoughts with which to move from the ideas discussed in Chapter 3:

- Labelling may not be a useful strategy
- Each of us is rational in our own world
- The environment in which an encounter occurs may be crucial.

What I am saying here is that, in thinking about how to deal with difficult people, it may be more productive to think about the **interaction** as being difficult than to put a label on another person and doom them to the 'difficult people in my life' category. It is not just them, it is also you, and the environment of the encounter that matters. This should be the focus of your thoughts and the target for your strategies. This new way of conceiving difficult people is illustrated in Figure 5.1.

FIGURE 5.1:   **A new model of difficult interactions**

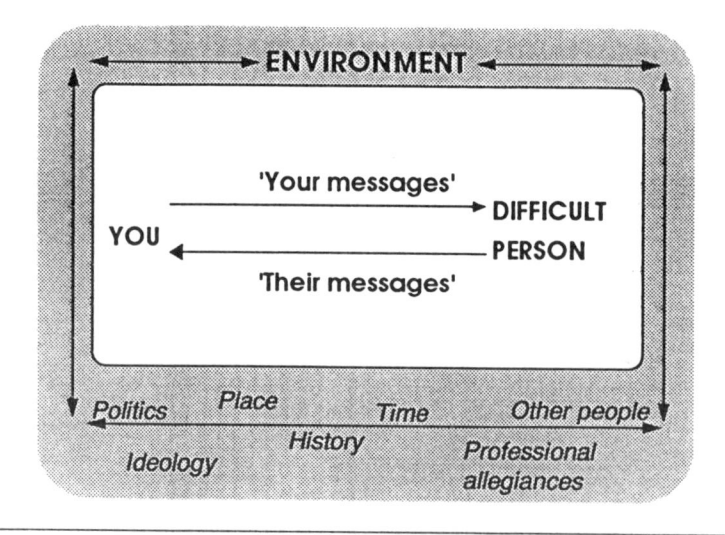

As Shotter (1995) observes in his book on the cultural politics of everyday life:

> *'What has been overlooked in modern psychology is that man is not simply a being immersed directly in nature, but is a being in a culture.'*

In the example above, risk depended on the speakers, the context in which the conversation occurred and the historical and political background to the discussion. For Inuit women risk is constructed through community experience. Statistical rates were meaningless in the local context - the occasional risks of childbirth are a natural part of life. For the doctor, however, risk in childbirth is an ongoing and frightening aspect of clinical life. Both parties failed to grasp the significance of each other's point of view. It is important that we attempt to put ourselves in the position of the other party to help us understand why the problem has arisen.

ACTIVITY:

Reflect on a group of people with whom you always seem to be in conflict. Daydream about what a typical day is like for these people - live it from the time they get up to the time they go to bed. Then, when you are well inside their character, imagine them meeting you in the corridor and the subsequent encounter that ensues.

You could more easily do this with a friend in a role playing exercise. What are your **gut reactions** when you play the 'difficult person'. Hopefully this will give you some insights, and allow you a greater degree of empathy with their position in future encounters.

Summary

The arguments raised here suggest that people cannot be ascribed certain predefined characteristics which easily lend themselves to the construction of counteractive strategies.

Labelling, although very neat and easy, may not be useful in our dealings with difficult people. We need to be more imaginative and understanding about why these difficult interactions occur. In other words, we need to adopt a new way of looking at the world that does not categorise and stigmatise others for our own convenient purposes.

This line of thought appears to contradict much of what is written concerning management skills where the emphasis is usually focused on the gain to you, as an individual, rather than the benefits to those with whom you work. Even where the ostensible aim is more towards the collective good, a very strong individualistic theme continues to prevail.

CHAPTER 6: DIFFICULT INTERACTIONS AND DEALING WITH THEM

Moving on from Individualism to Co-operation

Many psychologists believe that all behaviour is motivated by internal needs, and is learnt by reinforcement so that, for example, actions to, say, make relationships work better are governed by the costs and benefits involved. Ultimately we only act in our own self interests. Thus psychoanalytical theory reinforces the view that people should fulfil themselves and satisfy their own needs. This model of humans portrays an egotistical, selfish and non co-operative image where we each seek our individual rewards. There is, however, a great deal of evidence from recent research in social psychology to suggest that co-operation, working with others, is essential to human behaviour.

Argyle (1991) defines co-operation as 'acting together in a co-ordinated way at work, leisure or in social relationships in the pursuit of shared goals ...'. We can test the truth of this by observing the world around us. For example, the animal world provides many examples of co-operation, the warning signal, grooming others, etc.. Similarly, much has been written in sociology concerning communal relationships where there are close ties and concern for the welfare of others, *Gemeinschaft* relationships. However, it should not be imagined that individual needs are not sometimes met in such relationships. Doing work for charities, visiting the sick, whilst perceived as duties, may make us feel 'good' about ourselves or raise our standing within the community. Thus rather more self-centred objectives may govern such activities.

ACTIVITY:

Think of the people you work with. Pick out one who is a friend (i.e. someone you see a lot at work, take lunch with and so on), and a second who you dislike.

Now fill in the table below indicating how often you participate in certain activities with these two people.

	Friend at work	Disliked colleague
Discuss work		
Joke with them		
Discuss personal life		
Help other with work		
Ask for/give personal advice		
Tease them		
TOTAL		

Use some sort of scoring system, perhaps:

    4   very often

    3   at least once a day

    2   occasionally, once a day perhaps

    1   never

Which column had the highest score, the friend or the disliked colleague? A high score indicates a high degree of co-operation. It is probable that, the closer your relationship with your work colleague, the higher was your score and the more you co-operate with each other.

Such co-operation would be seen both in work-related activities, like taking on and seeing through a project, and also in social activities such as joking and teasing. People who 'play games' together have been shown to co-operate more and help each other over work matters.

There is a message here for our mission of learning how to deal with difficult people more effectively. Co-operation is essential. Even when you are in a situation of potential conflict, or where you feel the need to be assertive or to lead, it has been shown that co-operation is necessary. Leaders will only be followed if the followers believe that their leaders share their goals and will make every effort to attain them. Conflict situations are most effectively managed when there is concern for the goals of both sides, and a mutually beneficial solution can be arrived at.

The Significance of Context

The previous chapter considered the importance of the context in which interactions occurred and the way that the time, place or nature of an encounter could affect how people might react.

Although social psychology has had considerable impact on the way we understand people and what they do, many researchers have only studied subjects in total isolation. So people might be shown a film of social behaviour and then be asked who was responsible for what happened.

This type of research is rather sterile and, shorn of its social context, tends to miss out on crucial aspects such as:

- The effect of an audience
- The rules of agreed behaviour
- Shared concepts

Sometimes the importance of context and situation is obvious. A familiar example is the presence of the 'boss'. We have all seen the dramatic change in behaviour (both in ourselves and in others) when the immediate line manager or a more distant superior is present. Some people use the opportunity to score points, to emphasise the quality of their work or to stress the amount of time they are putting into the job. For others, the change in context results in a 'clamming up', a reluctance to say, or do, anything for fear of not coming up to scratch. In these obvious cases the importance of context is all too clear. However, most of us in our everyday lives fail to recognise its significance.

ACTIVITY: Consider this example.

I am making my way from the car park to a dental appointment. An elderly woman who is obviously distressed approaches asking for help. What will I do? Will I rush on to my appointment? Will I briefly acknowledge her request but quickly extricate myself? Will I enlist the help of a passer-by? Or will I ignore her?

Your probable answer to this question would be 'I can't possibly predict what you might do unless I have further information about you, your character, how you have acted in the past, or the sort of person you are'.

Am I generally a kind and considerate person, or am I well known for my callous attitudes? Am I a strong campaigner for the rights of older people, or do I think they are a drain on social resources?

But do you need this information about me as a **person**? In fact, research has shown that information about me as a person is of scant value in trying to predict my actions in advance (Ross and Nisbett, 1991). Our ability to predict how people will react in different situations is very limited.

> **ACTIVITY:**
>
> Reflect on the previous activity, and try to identify what information would be useful in predicting how I might react to the request for assistance?
>
> Some possible answers are provided below.

Most of the research evidence would suggest that situational factors, are more important than personality traits, in trying to judge any given outcome. So factors such as whether the woman was well-dressed, clean or drunk and who was observing the encounter or even whether it was early or late in the day may be relevant. How many women would stop at 6pm on a winter's evening in a badly lit car park? These are examples of the situational variables that crucially affect the way we interact with others.

Social context creates powerful forces which either provoke or constrain particular behaviours; so it is in our relationships with those we consider difficult. In these interactions it is important to try and unearth the context of the situation. Is it perhaps the situation, rather than any personally ingrained character trait, which is causing the difficulty?

> **ACTIVITY:**
> We all have our personal 'hit list'. Take whoever is at the top of it and, over the next month, keep a record of the difficult interactions that you endure with this person. Write them down as soon as possible after they have occurred. Where did they happen? When? What happened? Who else was there?
> At the end of the month pull out your diary of events and try to decide to what extent situational factors rather than personal characteristics influenced what happened.

In Place of the Other

Throughout the latter stages of this book I have repeatedly referred to the tendency with which we tend to look to our personal needs before those of others. In one sense this is understandable and may be linked to the strong thread of individualism that runs through Western culture. I have already mentioned how early psycho-analytical theory emphasised the importance of egotistical thinking to good mental health.

In addition, the first chapters of this book explored how many strategic management skills have been based on an individualistic viewpoint. We are taught from our earliest childhood to stand up for ourselves, and one of our most powerful cultural images is built around the gradual growth in independence that we experience on moving through child to adult-hood. Indeed, it is the very spectre of dependency that distresses so many of us as we consider old age.

To move forward in difficult relationships it may be necessary to stop focusing on our own needs (these are, after all, too obvious to our inner selves), and to start trying to see things through the eyes of others.

This argument would run counter to the model discussed in Chapter 3, whereby it is suggested that people can be categorised through their behaviour, and then be labelled ready for the counter-strategy. In fact, this type of labelling has been shown to be a self-fulfilling prophecy in some situations.

For example, in a now famous experiment conducted in 1968, investigators tested the IQ of school children and then shared the results with their teachers. Subsequently the researchers also alerted the teachers to certain children who, they suggested, could be expected to demonstrate substantial improvements in their IQ over the following year. These children did, indeed, tend to show the predicted improvement in IQ. However, the researchers had picked the children at random - there was no reason to suggest they were any more or any less likely than their classmates to improve and further studies showed that it was probably the way in which the 'chosen children' were treated by teachers that appeared to lead to the increase in IQ. In other words, teachers' expectations of pupils may affect their intellectual growth.

This seems to suggest that what we believe about a person may create a reality which confirms that belief - the self-fulfilling prophecy. If we label people then the label may indeed stick! Instead of labelling, categorising and acting on this information we should put our own thoughts and feeling to one side and truly listen to our difficult person. What are they trying to say to us? Why? How can we move towards a model of mutual co-operation?

Summary

This chapter has introduced some ideas that might help us to move beyond the traditional models of viewing interactions between people to a model based on co-operation. It explores the concept of co-operation and shows how this is crucial to effective relations and the way that social co-operation spills over into working co-operation.

Next we discussed the social context of encounters and how this might influence the outcome of an interaction between two people. How such factors as 'when', 'where' and 'how' an interaction occurs may have more influence on what happens than any particular traits of character of the people involved. Building on these two ideas, and those expressed in the previous chapter, led to the strategy of moving on. Moving on from individualism to a situation where we attempt to view events through the eyes of the beholder (i.e. putting ourselves 'in the place of the other').

CHAPTER 7: A PLAN FOR ACTION

There is obviously a multitude of ways through which the goals discussed in the previous chapter might be achieved. There is a tendency, in books such as this, to offer potential strategies through which an improvement in affairs might be achieved. This can be a problem since these strategies tend to be viewed as 'tablets of stone', the only way to move forward. If we can't achieve the desired goal, nothing changes or, if we don't have time in a busy work schedule to even think about strategies, let alone put them into practice, the whole project is abandoned. The approaches suggested here are, therefore, only outlines or 'skeletons' which you can change, modify or completely revise, but which could become your own way of dealing with things.

Listening Techniques

If you are really concerned to improve your interpersonal communication, and deal more effectively with so called difficult people, then an essential skill is that of listening. Most of us are lousy listeners! Listening attentively and uncritically is integral to building up relationships of trust and understanding and to moving difficult interactions into beneficial interactions. The most difficult aspect of listening is learning to keep quiet, not to butt in, not to interject with helpful suggestions or to provide your opinion too early.

Essentially there are three stages to successful listening:

- *Put yourself aside*: You need to forget about yourself and your own emotions. Anger, guilt, frustration or whatever, all need to be placed to one side. You may even find it useful to write your feelings down before the encounter. In other words, forget yourself and concentrate on the other party.

- *Check your understanding and clarify issues:* It is often necessary to check your understanding of what someone is saying to you. This can be done by paraphrasing the ideas you think you are hearing back to their owner (i.e. feed back to them the 'message' that you received). At this stage resist the temptation to add your own interpretation of what has been said.

  Clarification by the other party is often necessary before they can confirm that you are thinking along the same lines. You may have to paraphrase several times before understanding the true sense of what is being said is achieved.

- *Giving your own views:* This is a very tricky area and fraught with potential mine fields. While it is often feasible to provide factual information of your own this may be challenged and/or disregarded by the other party.

  Your opinions of the emotions or feelings that the other party may display should not be expressed. Peoples' feelings are their affair - not yours.

The goal of good listening should be more effective communication. Understanding is the basis of good relationships and, as we have seen, these relationships will act as the seed-corn for increased co-operation and more effective and mutual working practices.

This then is the basis of good listening, and there are already various models that implement these ideas. One such is **Synectics©**.

Synectics©

Synectics© (Synectics, 1991) is concerned with creative problem solving and, to achieve this, has developed techniques and meeting structures which, amongst other things, are designed to ensure:

- A better understanding of personal interactions
- The probability that everyone will leave a meeting feeling satisfied.

These objectives have obvious similarities with our task of trying to find effective ways of dealing with difficult interactions. The main avenue through which Synectics© achieves its goals is to make those thought processes that go on privately, explicit and public.

This approach is also very helpful in trying to see things through the eyes of others and is useful because it can help to provide solution-oriented ideas.

Our natural reaction to any new idea is to try to spot a flaw in it. The Synectics© process helps to prevent this by building on original ideas but in innovative ways and can capture the perspective of **both** participants in an encounter whilst preventing the demolition of ideas. This approach can, therefore, be very helpful in defusing encounters that might be difficult whilst building on ideas produced.

Synectics© have developed this approach as a sequence whereby:

- The positive aspects of any idea are expressed when it

is put forward

- A 'How to ....' statement is produced
- The thinking behind the statement is made clear and specific instead of being held hidden 'in the head' of the respondant.

The use of 'How to ....' statements is one of the central features of this approach. These are generated by participants in a group, in response to a 'client's' problem. The process can be modified for our purpose by asking the 'difficult' person to state the problem in hand. For instance, a problem such as 'To devise a way to deal with redundancies' can then be restated from our point of view by expressing it as a 'How to ....' statement. For example, in this case, 'How to reduce stress in individuals who may be made redundant' or 'How to ensure the prospects of redeployment are maximised.

The developmental thinking (or brainstorming) exercise, shown in Figure 7.1 (page 51), builds on this approach as a method of protecting ideas and those who have contributed them from destructive comments. The important features of this approach include:

- Commenting on how the idea might be useful or productive
- Indicating the direction to build on the idea 'What I need now is...'
- The thinking behind these comments (i.e. how the direction was decided upon).

FIGURE 7.1:   **The developmental thinking process**
[Modified from Synectics© (1991, p.20)]

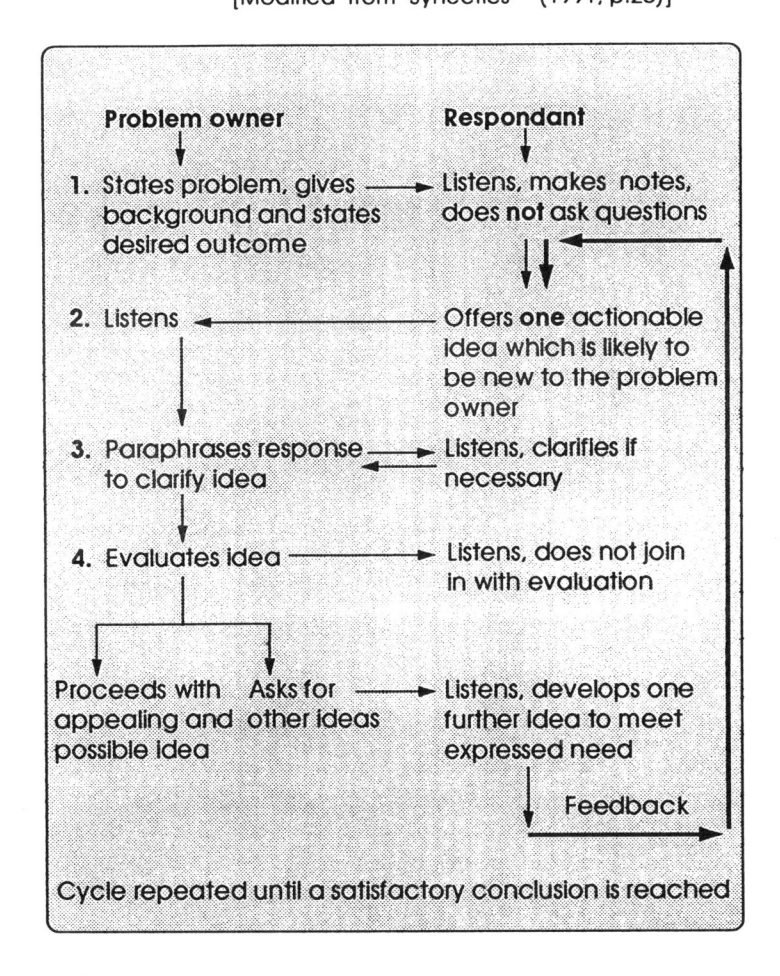

```
Problem owner                    Respondant
      ↓                               ↓
1. States problem, gives  ──→   Listens, makes notes,
   background and states        does not ask questions
   desired outcome                   ↓↓           ↑
                                                  │
2. Listens  ←───────────────    Offers one actionable
                                idea which is likely to
                                be new to the problem
      ↓                         owner

3. Paraphrases response  ──→    Listens, clarifies if
   to clarify idea       ←──    necessary
      ↓

4. Evaluates idea  ─────────→   Listens, does not join
      ↓                         in with evaluation
   ┌──┴──┐
   ↓     ↓
Proceeds with  Asks for  ──→   Listens, develops one
appealing and  other ideas     further idea to meet
possible idea                  expressed need
                                      ↓
                                   Feedback

Cycle repeated until a satisfactory conclusion is reached
```

The potential of this approach in dealing with interpersonal conflict is probably obvious. By using a formal structure in dealing with the interaction between two people it is possible to control more closely what happens. Things do not get out of hand, tempers are not lost and potentially useful solutions are produced. If handled well, each participant knows the boundary of his or her action. This approach, therefore, moves the difficult encounter from a position of mutual hostility to a more positive footing.

So, the next time you encounter a difficult situation, don't walk off in disgust or indulge in an argument. Take a deep breath and assertively ask your antagonist to try to identify both the nature of the problem and any positive aspects to your encounter and then you do the same. This positive approach should allow both of you to specify your needs and wishes for change.

Finally try to evaluate these ideas through the formalised sequence shown above. If the encounter has been exceptionally stormy you may need to attempt these new strategies after a 'cooling off period'.

A similar approach may be taken to consensus meetings where mutually acceptable courses of action are being sought. In this case, the conflict is broken down into a series of sub-problems linked with each of those involved. Solutions for these are again checked out using this technique and problem solving continues until an acceptable course of action is approved by all participants. The great advantages of this approach are:

- Its acknowledgment that a difficulty between two parties is actually a problem for both sides
- The process of taking each problem and party in turn facilitates the resolution of complex areas
- In the process of problem solving all ideas are valued - neither side feels bad
- Areas of disagreement are put into perspective

- Solutions are mutually developed and mutually accepted.

In order to demonstrate the effectiveness of the Synectics© approach it might be helpful to consider an example.

EXAMPLE:

Imagine that you have just undergone your annual appraisal with your boss. Despite the proliferation of this type of activity, and its claim to benefit both individuals and organisations alike, these exercises are seldom skilfully handled and, as a result, may be unpleasant for both appraiser and appraisee, a 'difficult' encounter. Your appraisal is no different; you emerge feeling marginally aggrieved but not really knowing why. Your boss is probably left with the impression that you are trying to be awkward but, again, he or she is not sure why. What went wrong?

In essence, the problem probably arose due to failure to realise exactly what you were saying to each the other; the difficulty of not making our private thoughts public recognised by Synectics©. Thus, when your boss suggests you should go on a public speaking course, you react with irritation (don't you already run the departmental meetings, present papers at conferences, etc.?). In reality, your boss may either have recognised some deficiency in your present performance, or may be grooming you for higher things. Perhaps he is impressed and thinks that, with some 'polishing' you could take his place at the next public committee meeting. If your respective thoughts are not made public you will never know what has motivated such comments.

If, as Synectics© suggests, the appraisal interview is constructed as a **two-way,** problem-solving exercise some of these difficulties would be avoided. The techniques outlined here allow the positive aspects of working together to be highlighted but, alongside this, the things you **both** wish you could change are identified. Both appraiser and appraisee can then seek solutions to improve these problems in the relationship. The responsibility for this is shared and both the appraiser and appraisee may need to make changes in their behaviour. In this way, genuine training needs and plans to address them will emerge.

Summary

This chapter has concentrated on two different, but related, strategies - listening techniques and Synectics©. It has explored how these may be used to improve the way we interact with others, in both individuals and groups.

CHAPTER 8: CONCLUSIONS

Guides that have been developed to help people to improve and promote their management skills often provide practical guidance in an authoritative tone. They sometimes suggest there is only one way to go about things, and seldom offer any background research or theory to underpin the advice dispensed within their covers.

Although such books are often easy to read, and the exercises fun to complete, they frequently oversimplify matters. Furthermore the thoughtful reader is left with little more than a list of instructions, with very little in the way of explanation or understanding. This text has tried to avoid some of these pitfalls.

While not pretending to have provided the complete and authoritative guide on dealing with difficult interactions, I have attempted to ensure that the information and suggestions provided here are supported by the relevant theory and to give a deeper insight into this fascinating area of human interaction.

In pursuing this goal I have, therefore, presented not only some strategies for action, but also some flavour of the research that goes alongside them. Two particular world views, and a conglomerate of theoretical perspectives, drawn from anthropology, behavioural psychology and social psychology, have been offered and we have examined how difficult interactions might be explored through these different routes.

Stemming from these have come strategies that might facilitate a move towards improving difficult encounters, a menu of ideas and strategies from which to choose. Consider the rationale and evidence behind each, and decide on the course of action that best suits you.

At this point you might like to tackle what I consider to be both a common and a difficult problem - the democratic dictatorship. Yes, I did say that labelling might not be helpful, but in this case the label quickly conveys to you what I have in mind.

The case of the democratic dictatorship concerns the situation where ostensibly we are consulted and our opinions are sought concerning a problem but, in reality, the decision(s) have already been made and nothing that we say, or do will alter them.

This hierarchical style of management is widespread, and Lupton (1986), in an excellent critique, suggests that, while managers would say that they consult widely and take the views of their staff into account, in reality it is the managers who make the decisions. The staff are excluded.

In recent years there seems to have been a great reluctance by managers of all levels to impose their decisions openly, to simply say 'I have decided what will be done'. While this is certainly undemocratic, at least you and your colleagues know the truth of the situation. You may not like, or agree with, the decision, but at least you are under no illusion as to how it was arrived at.

In the democratic dictatorship, managers may indulge in a considerable degree of empty and worthless discussion with the intention of trying to implant their ideas from the 'bottom up'. This is simply a facade of democracy. You are being given an opportunity to contribute to the debate but, in reality, little notice will be taken of what you say. Sometimes this ploy is all too obvious but, occasionally, it is very difficult to spot. Recognition apart, this is still a very perverse situation to deal with effectively, and one that causes much 'bad blood'.

> **ACTIVITY:**
>
> Imagine yourself to be in a meeting where a democratic dictator is in full swing. Either role play this with a friend or colleague or go through the process in your head.
>
> Once you are 'on the stage' try some of the strategies suggested in this book and see how well they work. Is it useful to label the perpetrator - the democratic dictator?
>
> Recognise their characteristics, know when they are coming and where they are coming from, and have your strategy ready. What do you think the outcome might be?
>
> How does it work out when you role play the situation? Try an effective listening session or the approach suggested by Synectics©.
>
> Which of these methods works most effectively for you?

The idea of self-reflection was first mentioned in Chapter 1. Self-reflection on work practices can engender a cycle in which we observe what we do, reflect on our actions, consider alternative modes of action, and then test these approaches to see which is most effective. This type of reflective practice is common in some professions, such as nursing and teaching. It is based on the philosophy that reflection on the conditions and reasons that influence both our actions and reactions can lead to emancipation and greater knowledge, to becoming an autonomous agent of change through our own actions.

By reading this text and trying out the activities you have begun the process of reflection. By using your experience you can move forward towards your personal model for dealing more effectively with 'difficult' people.

REFERENCES

Argyle, M., 1989, *The Social Psychology of Work*, Penguin, Harmondsworth.

Argyle, M., 1991, *Co-operation. The Basis of Sociability*, Routledge, London.

Bransom, R., 1981, *Coping with Difficult People*, Ballantine Books, New York.

Department of Health and Social Security, 1983, *NHS Management Inquiry*, (The Griffiths' Report) DA(83)38, DHSS, London.

Lupton, T., 1986), *Organisational change: top down or bottom up management*. In: Maynon-White, W. (Editor) *Planning and Managing Change*, Harper and Row, London.

Markham, U. , 1993, *How to Deal with Difficult People*, Thorsons, London.

Ross, L. and Nisbett, R. E. , 1991, *The Person and the Situation*, McGraw Hill Inc., New York.

Shotter, J., 1993, *Cultural Politics of Everyday Life*, Open University Press, Buckingham.

Synectics©, 1991, *Synectics: Helping to Change the Way Organisations Think, Work, and Behave*, Synectics Ltd, Hemel Hempstead.

FURTHER READING

Bone, D., 1988, A Practical Guide to Effective Listening, Kogan Page, London. *A very practical short guide with numerous self completion exercises.*

Chapman, M., 1994, Social anthropology and business studies - mutual benefit? Anthropology in Action, 1, 12-15. *A paper discussing the development of business academia and the part which anthropology might play towards a new conceptualisation based more on naturalism than positivism.*

Fogel, A., 1993, Developing through Relationships, Harvester Wheatsheaf, London. *Explains how humans develop through their relationships with others. Focuses on communication and different relationships, such as those between adults or adult-child. Encompasses a wide range of disciplines. Academic but quite accessible.*

Hastorf, A. H., Schneider, D. J. and Polefka, J., 1970, Person Perception, Addison-Wesley Publishing Co. London. *Designed for those with no prior knowledge this text discusses social perception (i.e. the factors affecting the way we see others). Very factual but not difficult to understand. A good book for those wanting a more 'in-depth' knowledge.*

Pennington, D. C., 1986, Essential Social Psychology, Edward Arnold, London. *An introduction to the different aspects of social psychology*

Schon, D. A., 1983, The Reflective Practitioner, Basic Books, New York. *Explores the puzzle of the relationship between academic and professional knowledge. 'The best professionals know more than they can put into words'. A valuable and original insight into how reflection on our actions occurs. Meaty but fascinating stuff and quite easy to read.*

WHY NOT TRY ANOTHER ASSET BOOK?

Other titles include:

'To thine own self be true': a guide to assertiveness in the workplace

Sue Holmes

Unfairly treated? Difficulty in standing up for your point of view? Want to change the situation? A step-by-step consideration of how problems arise and how they can be overcome

Stress management: guide to coping with stress

Kevin Gournay

More people are suffering from stress than ever before and suffering a wider range of secondary symptoms.
Identify its causes and effects. Find wide-ranging and comprehensive advice in this helpful text. Manage the symptoms and overcome its deleterious effects.

Communication for purpose

Graham Rawlinson

Effective communication is critical to human relationships - at home and at work. Do you always tell your partner what you really mean? Do you always 'get your message across'?
If not, read this book. Graham Rawlinson has spent most of his working life helping people to overcome these problems.
Can he help you?

Price: £5.95 each + £1.00 post and packing for each order

ASSET BOOKS
Practical solutions to everyday problems

AVAILABLE FROM: ASSET BOOKS LTD (Dept M), PO Box 36, Leatherhead, Surrey KT22 8YG. Tel: 01372-372142.